MW01196877

IMAGES
of America

WATKINS

THE WATKINS CITY
A GROUP VIEW OF THE WATKINS HOME OFFICE BUILDINGS, BANK
FACTORIES, BRANCHES AND PRINTING PLANT.

This 1920s Watkins advertisement depicts various Watkins manufacturing and distribution centers found throughout the United States, repositioned to appear as if they are near the Watkins Administration Building in downtown Winona, Minnesota.

IMAGES
of America

WATKINS

Watkins Incorporated

ARCADIA

Copyright © 2004 by Watkins Incorporated
ISBN 0-7385-3310-6

Published by Arcadia Publishing
Charleston SC, Chicago IL, Portsmouth NH, San Francisco CA

Printed in Great Britain

Library of Congress Catalog Card Number: 2004108336

For all general information contact Arcadia Publishing at:
Telephone 843-853-2070
Fax 843-853-0044
E-mail sales@arcadiapublishing.com
For customer service and orders:
Toll-Free 1-888-313-2665

Visit us on the internet at http://www.arcadiapublishing.com

Mr. and Mrs. R.D. Salmon stand beside their Dodge truck with a custom-made product carrier.

CONTENTS

ACKNOWLEDGMENTS

Watkins Incorporated would like to thank John Goplen for selecting the photographs and illustrations, and for writing the captions that accompany them. Watkins would also like to thank the Winona County Historical Society for their help in providing photographs found in this book. Special thanks go to Dave Fricke, Jim Welch, Sandy Moger, Eloyce Schindler, and Esther Bescup of Watkins Incorporated for sharing their knowledge of Watkins history and answering the many questions that arose during the creation of this book. And a special thank you to Maura Brown of Arcadia Publishing for her help and patience with getting this book to print.

The following have provided permission to reprint their photographs in this book: the Winona County Historical Society and George Carrell Jr.

Watkins dessert mixes, baking products, and spices were top sellers for the company during the mid-1930s.

INTRODUCTION

The J.R. Watkins Company began in a back room of a small house in Plainview, Minnesota, in 1868. In 1885 Joseph Ray Watkins moved his company to Winona, Minnesota, located on the Mississippi River. At the time, Winona was one of Minnesota's largest cities and a major transportation hub for both railroad and river traffic. Winona had several large sawmills and employed hundreds of men who could benefit from using Watkins Liniment on their sore muscles after a hard day at the mills. J.R. was so confident in the benefits of his liniment that he introduced the "Trial Mark" bottle and money-back guarantee. In 1893 the first branch office was opened in San Francisco, California, and the J.R. Watkins Company went from a regional to a national company. In 1915 Watkins became an international business when it opened a branch in Winnipeg, Canada. By the 1920s the J.R. Watkins Company was the largest direct selling company in the world, reaching its peak of success after World War II. The company then began a period of slow decline that would last 25 years and end with the company filing for bankruptcy in 1978. The company was sold to a self-made businessman, Irwin Jacobs, who still saw the potential for success in the company. The next 25 years would see a rebirth of Watkins and a return to profitability.

The long, rich history of Watkins will be illustrated through photographs, postcards, advertising memorabilia, and other visual sources in this book. Through these materials, the book will illustrate just how large Watkins was at its height of success by showing manufacturing plants, distribution centers, and stores that spanned across the North American continent, Australia, New Zealand, South Africa, and Great Britain. The distinctiveness and diversity found at each Watkins location—and in the people who worked manufacturing and selling Watkins products—will be brought out in each image.

American culture and society have long been transformed by the advancement of technology. Manufacturing, marketing, and the distribution of Watkins products have evolved over the past 135 years as a result of these advancements. Examples of these changes include: the transition from the horse and buggy to the automobile, the use small contract delivery services to deliver Watkins products to a customer, the use of the Internet instead of large advertising posters, and the use of automation over human labor at manufacturing plants and distribution centers.

Watkins played a very important economic and social role in the development of the city of Winona, where the company is still headquartered. It was not only the largest employer in the city, but it also brought in tens of thousands of people to tour the company's general offices, manufacturing plant, and research farm. Today tourists still come and visit the Watkins Administration Building and Museum. The Winona National & Savings Bank (once referred to as the Watkins Bank) and the Paul Watkins Home (currently a nursing home) are points of interest on the Historic Walking Tour offered by the Winona County Historical Society. Watkins was the largest contributor to Winona's first Winter Carnival in 1923 and continues this civic tradition by sponsoring such events as the 2004 Grand Excursion and Winona's Shakespeare Festival.

The J.R. Watkins Company gave these six automobiles away as prizes during the 1937 Liniment Contest.

One
J.R. WATKINS

Joseph Ray Watkins transformed a small business into the world's largest direct selling company, making a lasting impact on both American entrepreneurism and the city of Winona, Minnesota.

Joseph Ray Watkins was born near Cincinnati, Ohio, on August 21, 1840. He was the son of Benjamin and Sophronia Keeler Watkins. J.R. moved from Ohio to Stearns County, Minnesota, in 1862. In 1868 he moved to Plainview, Minnesota, and shortly thereafter, he secured the rights to manufacture and sell a liniment formula created by Dr. Richard Ward. (Courtesy of the Winona County Historical Society.)

J.R. Watkins founded the J.R. Watkins Medical Company in a back room of his house at Plainview, Minnesota, in 1868.

Mary Ellen Herberling married J.R. Watkins on September 10, 1868, at Short Creek, Ohio. The young couple moved to Plainview, Minnesota, in the winter of 1868. Mary and J.R. would have two children, Grace Eleanor Watkins and George Benjamin Watkins. Mary Ellen died on April 15, 1904, after a brief week-long illness. (Courtesy of the Winona County Historical Society.)

This 1891 photograph shows J.R. Watkins (third from the right wearing a top hat) posing for a picture with Watkins salesmen in front of the original Watkins Manufacturing Plant in Winona, Minnesota. J.R.'s daughter, Grace, is standing in the window next to an unidentified man.

After Mary Ellen Watkins died, Grace Watkins would often accompany J.R. to social and family gatherings. Here Grace, second from the left, and J.R., far right, pose with unidentified family members.

Family was very important to J.R. Watkins. His daughter, Grace, married E.L. King in 1904, and in September of 1911, J.R. married E.L.'s mother, Martha King. This image shows J.R. sitting on his lawn with Martha King, his granddaughter, Mary Eleanor King, and son-in-law, E.L. King, who was also his stepson.

J.R. Watkins is pictured with his granddaughter, Mary Eleanor King.

Like many of the successful men of his era, J.R. Watkins was a man of vision not only in manufacturing and sales but also in regard to the impending changes in American society. In this picture, J.R. and his family are pulling his old carriage behind their automobile as they come off of the High Wagon Bridge at the end of Main Street in Winona, Minnesota.

As his business grew, J.R. began to travel farther away from the Midwest. In May of 1908, J.R. took his family on a vacation to southern California. He is pictured here sitting for a photograph next to a stuffed penguin at a photographer's studio at Ocean Park near San Diego.

At a time when the preferred methods of long distance travel were by train or ship, J.R. Watkins would often travel by automobile. Here J.R. and his chauffeur pause to have their picture taken while on one of their many road trips.

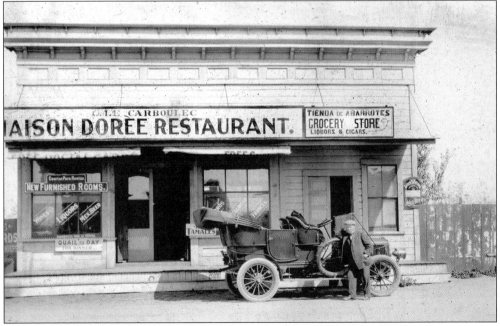

Vacations to far-away places offered more than relaxation—they also offered a chance to visit potential new markets for Watkins products. In this image, J.R. poses in front of the Maison Doree Restaurant and Grocery Store in southern California. Note that the signs are in both Spanish and English.

When J.R. was not traveling overseas or across the United States, he would travel around Winona County in his new automobile. At the beginning of the 20th century, country roads were often nothing more than dirt trails, but that did little to deter the growing number of automobiles. Here J.R. Watkins and his chauffer stop on Stockton Hill, just outside of Winona, to have their photograph taken.

Two

THE EARLY YEARS

In 1885, Winona was a booming lumber town of 20,000 people. Its location on the upper Mississippi River made it an important transportation center that was served by three major railroads and heavy steamboat traffic. This made Winona the logical choice when J.R. decided to relocate his growing business from Plainview, Minnesota. (Courtesy of the Winona County Historical Society.)

In the 1880 U.S. Census, Emmett Carrell is listed as a traveling agent living at the J.R. Watkins household in Plainview, Minnesota. Carrell is believed to be one of the earliest Watkins salesmen, if not the first. His territory included the towns of Zumbrota and Wabasha, Minnesota. In 1907, Carrell moved to Zumbrota where he continued to sell Watkins products. He died in 1928. (Courtesy of George Carrell Jr.)

18

By the turn of the century, the J.R. Watkins Company was expanding so rapidly that it needed to add a new building to its manufacturing complex every two years. This is the view looking west on the corner of 4th and Chestnut Streets. Even with these large four-story buildings, the company was continually running out of space.

For the first 50 years of the company's life, rural sales dominated the company's business. Here is a photograph of C.A. Johnson of Alexandria, Minnesota, standing in front of his home in 1890. The "Watkins Men" not only sold quality household products; they often brought news and local gossip to the farm families of rural America.

Beginning in the early 1920s, Watkins decided to expand its sales into urban America. A separate City Sales Department was created at this time. In this early 1940s photograph of the City Sales Department, the many clerks can be seen updating and filing the records of thousands of Watkins City Sales dealers.

Just about any household product could be obtained from the local Watkins Man. Shown here are Watkins Allspice, Watkins Dandruff Remover Scalp Tonic, and Watkins Pepper.

In the late 19th century, the main form of advertising for the J.R. Watkins Medical Company came from the Watkins salesmen. Their wagons and buggies were easily identified by the Watkins name painted on them.

J.R. Watkins was a "hands-on" businessman. This image shows his car parked in front of the home of a rural Watkins dealer whom he has stopped to visit. The sign on the front porch reads "Watkins Remedies."

As the company's sales grew, so did the variety of products offered by the J.R. Watkins Medical Company. By 1895, an assortment of spices and extracts were being sold. Here are two early examples of Watkins spice tins.

Work began on the new Watkins Administration Building in 1911. The building was designed by Chicago architect George Washington Maher and constructed out of concrete and steel with a limestone exterior. J.R. Watkins' original two-story brick headquarters can be seen on the far left of the photograph.

As beautiful as the new Administration Building was on the outside, it was even more impressive on the inside. The interior features veined Italian marble and yellow Sienna marble. There are 224 Tiffany stained glass ceiling windows that cover 3,201 square feet, 22 specially designed concrete and steel bowl ceiling lights, and the rotunda ceiling is surfaced with mosaic tile laid in a pattern using gold inlaid tile to accent the designs.

By 1913, the J.R. Watkins Company occupied an entire city block and was still faced with a shortage of space. Once again the company turned to architect George Washington Maher for help. Maher designed a ten-story manufacturing plant located behind the Administrative Building on the site of J.R.'s original two-story brick headquarters.

The new Watkins Manufacturing Plant contained modern equipment that allowed the company to meet the high demand for its products. This photograph shows dry ingredients being dumped from mixers onto paper-lined carts.

In 1913, the J.R. Watkins Company was growing both within the city of Winona and beyond its borders. Besides designing Watkins' new manufacturing plant in Winona, Chicago architect George Washington Maher also designed the new Watkins Warehouse and Manufacturing Plant in Memphis, Tennessee.

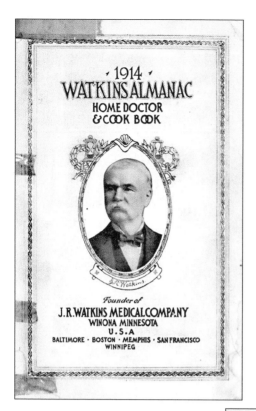

J.R. Watkins understood the importance of marketing his products, and as a result, he built one of the largest printing operations west of the Mississippi. Millions of pieces of printed literature were produced, ranging from advertising and company newspapers to calendars, cookbooks, and almanacs like the 1914 Watkins Almanac, shown here.

The Watkins printing operation contained modern, state-of-the-art equipment as seen in this photograph of a Watkins employee typing the Canadian Roll of Honor on a Linus Machine.

By the early 1920s, the once-familiar Watkins wagons were being replaced by specially-modified Ford Model Ts. Texas Watkins dealer Fred Hooks is seen here standing in front of his Watkins delivery trucks.

Watkins played a prominent role in Winona's first Winter Carnival in February of 1922. The *Winona Republican-Herald* newspaper gave the following description of Watkins' participation in the opening parade: "The largest costumed delegation in the parade was that of the J.R. Watkins Co. Led by the Elks Fife and Drum Corps, this delegation was grouped off into fifteen different sections, each one representing a department of the plant. Varied and diverse were the costumes, some expensive and some made by the marchers. All were pretty."

The J. R. Watkins Co. Diamond Ball Team, City Champions, 1926

Teamwork has always been one of the cornerstones of success at Watkins, both on and off the field.

Three

EXPANSION INTO AN INTERNATIONAL COMPANY

This composite view of the "Watkins City" exemplifies the development of the company as it began to expand beyond the borders of the United States.

In 1913 the J.R. Watkins Company became an international company when it opened a new manufacturing plant in Winnipeg, Canada. This plant would help meet the growing demand for Watkins products in Canada. Within a few years, new branches would be opened in Montreal, Quebec City, and Vancouver.

In the years following the death of J.R. Watkins, the company began to expand the variety of products it sold. The result was to take the J.R. Watkins Company from a national to a worldwide company. Shown here in this 1920 product photograph are Watkins Prepared Mustard, Watkins Cloves, Watkins Cinnamon, and Watkins Red Pepper.

Corked bottles were a hold-over from an earlier era of manufacturing. They eventually disappeared during the early 1920s as modern manufacturing equipment was introduced at the manufacturing plant in Winona, Minnesota.

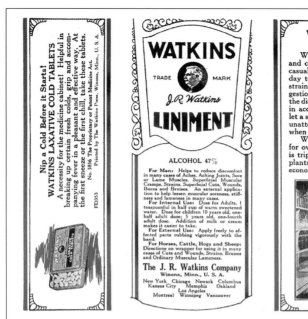

Watkins Liniment has been a top seller for Watkins for over 135 years. Over time, uses for the liniment have changed. This 1929 advertisement promotes the use of the liniment for relief from internal ailments. The internal use of Watkins Liniment would be the subject of two major lawsuits against Watkins by the federal government. The company lost both suits and changed all labels and advertisements to restrict its use to external use only.

As the American economic boom of the 1920s began, the company began to produce its first perfumes and cosmetic products. Shown in this 1920 photograph are Watkins Belle De Nuit Talc, Watkins Belle De Nuit Perfume, Watkins Garda Talcum, and Watkins Garda Nail Polish.

After becoming president of the J.R. Watkins Company upon Paul Watkins' death in 1931, E.L. King Sr. began rapidly expanding the company into overseas markets. In 1935 Watkins opened a branch office in Melbourne, Australia. Here members of the City Sales Department stand for a picture outside their Melbourne office in 1940.

The J.R. Watkins Company was the world's largest direct selling company by the 1930s, and it was also Winona's largest employer. During the Great Depression, Watkins offered good jobs when millions were unemployed. Hundreds of people worked in the Administration Building and Manufacturing Plant, which encompassed a whole city block, during the 1930s.

Although the "Watkins Man" was familiar all across the United States, the social changes brought about by the Great Depression were beginning to change the face of the Watkins company. In order to help support the family, women were beginning to seek work outside the home. Pictured here are Mrs. L.C. Longley, Miss Ollie Ezill, Mrs. E.W. Chapman, Mrs. J.S. Keyes, Mrs. W.J. Barber, and Mrs. Bertie Hartman, all Watkins dealers from Chattanooga, Tennessee.

By continuing to expand despite a worldwide depression in the 1930s, Watkins earned the reputation of being a "depression-proof" company. In 1937 Watkins opened a new branch office in Vancouver, British Columbia.

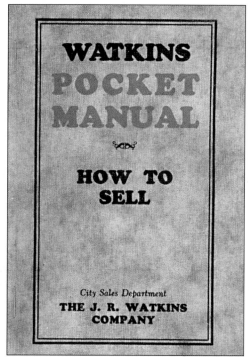

With 60 years of direct selling experience, the company had developed a very detailed and effective selling program for its salesmen. The program was specifically structured towards either Rural Sales or City Sales depending on the territory that each salesman covered.

Watkins manufactured products that were sought after by both rural and city customers.

The success of the J.R. Watkins Company would not have been possible without the hundreds of thousands of Watkins dealers that have sold its products since 1868. Pictured in this 1930 photograph is L.T. Adell, a Watkins dealer from California, with his two grandsons, Norman Frantz and Bobbie Frantz.

The 1933 World's Fair in Chicago offered Watkins the opportunity to display its hundreds of products to people from all over the world. Eventually, Watkins would establish branches in Australia, New Zealand, South Africa, Canada, and Great Britain.

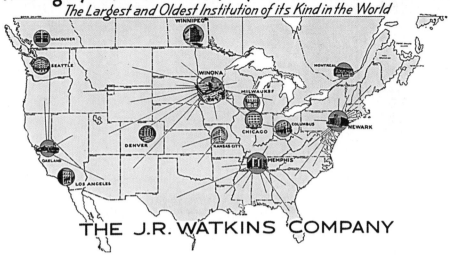

The Mighty $10,000,000 Company Behind Watkins Products
The Largest and Oldest Institution of its Kind in the World

THE J.R. WATKINS COMPANY

Sixty-Five Years of Progress

The World's Fair marks a century of progress for the city of Chicago. It dramatizes mankind's forward movement and shows the progress of invention, science and industry in the hundred years since the founding of Chicago.

The World's Fair also marks 65 years of progress for The J. R. Watkins Company. It was, therefore, fitting that the largest and oldest institution of its kind in the world should be represented at the Chicago World's Fair. There are four displays in four of the most famous buildings as illustrated on the inside of this folder.

It was back in 1868 that the House of Watkins was founded on a new idea of organized distribution that would bring the products of the manufacturer direct to the customer, thereby eliminating the expenses and profits of middlemen. Bound with this idea was the determination of the founder that only highest quality products should carry the name of Watkins.

For over three generations this ideal has been zealously guarded until now in every state and in every province of the North American Continent, housewives have found that the name "J. R. Watkins" stands unalterably for high quality and honest value.

North, South, East, or West—no matter where you live, the helping hand of this gigantic institution brings the world's choicest markets to your doorstep. This institution has grown until today it is the largest and the oldest of its kind in the world.

There are 9,000 dealers delivering Watkins Products direct to the consumer from 36 great factories and branches strategically located to give you fresher products and faster service at saving prices.

By 1933, Watkins was the largest and oldest direct selling company in the world. In the United States, Watkins branches and salesman could be found in every state.

In 1933, E.L. King Sr. hired C.P. (Cy) Crawford to convert a 300-acre farm on Homer Ridge into a research farm. The farm was later expanded to almost 1,200 acres. Under Crawford's management, the farm became a showplace for the demonstration of animal nutrition experiments.

The introduction of new items was not limited to cooking and cleaning products; perfumes, colognes, and cosmetics were also introduced. In the mid-1930s, Watkins launched the Mary King Cosmetics line. Named after J.R. Watkins' granddaughter, Mary Eleanor King, this line was marketed as upscale and glamorous.

This Free Offer Brings Summer Comfort

with hair health and beauty within your reach

No Charge for this Remarkable Deodorant Powder

Mary King Deodorant Powder gives you a safe and sure means to guard against perspiration and resulting offensive odors. It is pure white and delicately perfumed and contains ingredients which neutralize the perspiration and absorb the moisture, thus protecting the clothes. If you are troubled with perspiring feet, you will find this powder a great aid.

Use it liberally over the entire body and you never need fear offending.

DEODORANT POWDER

FREE to Every Customer!

Watkins wants every woman to have the advantage of these three remarkable summer beauty preparations. For a limited time only your Watkins Dealer will bring you a beautiful full-sized package of Mary King Deodorant Powder Free with the purchase of Watkins 18-oz. Cocoanut Oil Shampoo and Watkins Lemon Lotion. Even at the regular price these products cost you but a fraction of what you might pay elsewhere. If you value your appearance, this Special Offer gives you a bargain you can't afford to overlook.

YOUR WATKINS DEALER

AN971-534-1MM-2663   PRINTED IN U. S. A.

These Products Will Make a Big Difference in your Appearance

Summer time is hard on the hair. The heat, perspiration, dust and the natural oily secretion from the scalp form a film that is difficult to remove. The regular use of Watkins Cocoanut Oil Shampoo, however, will keep the scalp clean and healthy and the hair soft and lustrous. Preserve the beauty of your hair. It is woman's greatest charm.

Watkins Lemon Lotion will provide that needed summer protection against red, chapped and sunburned hands and skin. It has a softening and whitening effect.

Beginning in the 1930s, Watkins marketed its Mary King cosmetics and perfumes as glamorous and essential for any woman, as depicted in this 1930s advertisement.

In the age before television, the Internet, and telemarketing, the automobile allowed Watkins dealers to remain independent. Delivery automobiles served as offices, warehouses, and advertising billboards to thousands of Watkins salesmen during the mid-20th century. Here Watkins dealers from Kentucky and Tennessee stand beside their delivery cars and trucks.

This 1939 photograph shows a display of Watkins Mouth Wash, Brushless Cream, Tooth Paste, Antiseptic, and Shaving Cream. Displays such as this were often seen in the front windows of Watkins counter stores.

At its peak, Watkins had 137 counter stores throughout the United States. These counter stores were not only used as retail stores, but also as distribution centers and training centers for Watkins salesmen. Pictured here is the Seattle branch office and counter store.

During the Christmas season of 1940, an abundance of Watkins products became available to consumers. The Washington D.C. counter store offered Christmas gifts for under the tree and ingredients to make delicious holiday meals.

The Watkins Company was an early pioneer of equal opportunities for women and minorities. These salesmen and women brought Watkins products into new households, helping to expand the market for all products manufactured by Watkins.

Four
THE FAMILY

J.R. Watkins sits on the steps of his porch with his daughter, Grace, and E.L. King, along with the brother and sister of E.L. King. Pictured in the front, from left to right are: Grace Watkins King, E.L. King, and Maude King. Sitting in the back are J.R. Watkins, unidentified, and C.L. King.

The tradition of manufacturing and selling quality products begun by J.R. Watkins in 1868 is still being carried out 136 years later—as is the tradition of putting his portrait on product labels.

This house at 206 East Broadway in Winona was the home of J.R. Watkins and his family. After J.R. died in 1911, his second wife, Martha King Watkins, continued to live here until her death in 1925. The house was later torn down, but the carriage house remains.

Grace Watkins, on the far right, has her photograph taken with Paul and Florence Watkins, along with two of their children, Roderick and Florence, and Paul's mother, Julia Watkins. This photo was taken on the porch of J.R. Watkins' home at 206 East Broadway.

Roderick Watkins was the son of Paul and Florence Watkins and enjoyed the privileges that went along with the family wealth. Paul was a graduate of the Carnegie Institute of Technology and Harvard University. He worked for the J.R. Watkins Company until 1937, when he retired from the postition of President of the Watkins Maryland branch. Here is Paul, on the right, as a teenager with friends swimming near the Minne-o-wah Club near Homer, Minnesota.

Born in Plainview, Minnesota, Grace Watkins was the only surviving child of J.R. and Mary Watkins. After J.R.'s death in 1911, Grace became the largest stockholder in Watkins and would remain as such until her death in 1975 at age 98.

Ernest Leroy King was born to Charles and Martha Salsman King in 1879, at Gallipolis, Ohio. While working as a typewriter salesman in New York City, he met Grace Watkins and they began dating. They were married on November 19, 1904.

Mary Eleanor King, the first child of E.L. and Grace King, is shown here with her father. She would later lend her name to a successful line of cosmetics that the J.R. Watkins Company sold as Mary King Cosmetics.

"Bud" King was born E.L. King Jr. in 1914 to Ernest and Grace King. Bud would enjoy all the benefits of being born into wealth. He would also be left with the expectation of running the company when he grew up.

Built by Winona Machine & Boat Works
For E. L. King, Winona, Minn.

The wealth from the success of the J.R. Watkins Company afforded the family many luxuries not available to the general population during the early 1900s. Here is a post card of E.L. King's speedboat named after his daughter.

E.L. King Sr. was very impressed with the architectural works of George W. Maher, the designer of the Watkins Administration Building, and so hired him to design a summer home for his family. Situated beneath two large limestone bluffs and overlooking the Mississippi River just south of Homer, Minnesota, the new home was called Rockledge.

Although Rockledge was less than five miles from Winona, the primitive roads of the early 20th century made even short trips an adventure. Here is what the future U.S. Highway 61 looked like in the early 1900s. This section of road is just south of Homer. The bluffs around Trempealeau, Wisconsin, can be seen in the distance.

In this photograph, Bud, E.L., and Grace stand on the terrace at Rockledge.

Rockledge was a beautiful home whose furnishings were also specifically designed by George W. Maher. During the 1930s, the home would be remodeled in the Art Deco style that was popular at the time. For nearly 70 years, the home mirrored both the success and decline of Watkins Company and the King Family. The home was abandoned after the family lost control of Watkins Products Incorporated in 1978, and was torn down by Bud King shortly before his death in 1987.

Often referred to as the Watkins Bank, the Winona National & Savings Bank was formed by E.L. King and Paul Watkins. Both men would serve as president of the bank, followed by E.L. King Jr. The Egyptian Revival structure was designed by George W. Maher and completed in 1916.

The Paul and Florence Watkins home at 175 East Wabasha Street was designed Ralph Adams Cram and was built between 1924 and 1928. Paul and Florence furnished this house with antique furniture, artwork, and tapestries from all over Europe. The Great Hall featured a pipe organ that had 5,975 pipes and a Steinway concert grand piano. After Florence died in 1956, the family donated the house to a Methodist group so that it could become a nursing home. Today it is known as Watkins Manor. (Courtesy of the Winona County Historical Society.)

In 1924, Bud King accompanied his parents on their first African safari. He is shown here with a zebra that he has just shot. Many of the animals taken during their safaris to Africa were stuffed and put on display at the Winona National & Savings bank where they can still be viewed today.

In 1927, Mary Eleanor King married Ralph Boalt in an elegant ceremony on the grounds of Rockledge. As a wedding gift to their daughter, E.L. and Grace King commissioned Philip Maher, the son of George Maher, to design and construct a brick Chateau next to the grounds of Rockledge.

Over the years, only a handful of people became inner circle friends with the King family. One such couple was Fred and Mary Jackson. Fred was the vice-president and general manager of the Owl Motor Company from 1930 to 1961. Owl Motors was a Ford dealership owned by E.L. King Sr. and Bud King. Here Fred and Mary have their picture taken on the west lawn of Rockledge with Mary Eleanor King, her husband, Ralph Boalt, and his dog, Artus.

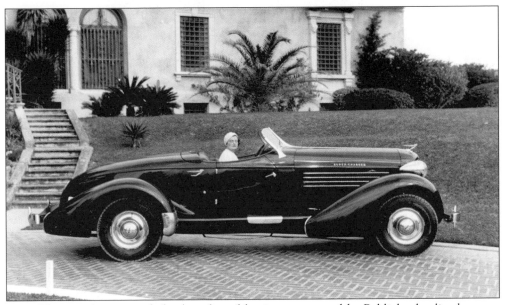

Mary Eleanor also enjoyed the benefits of having great wealth. Publicly she lived a very glamorous lifestyle and she would use that image to help promote and sell her Mary King Cosmetics Line, introduced by Watkins in the mid-1930s. She is shown sitting in her supercharged luxury roadster outside her Florida home.

The family often enjoyed outings and vacations to their various properties throughout the United States. In this 1938 photograph, Grace and E.L. King Sr. are sitting on a log with their daughter in-law, Neill Meginnis King, and family friend, Mary Jackson. The picture was taken at Queens Bluff near the present-day Twin Bluffs between Winona, Minnesota, and La Crosse, Wisconsin.

E.L. King, often referred to as "The Chief," enjoyed visiting with Watkins dealers from around the country whenever he traveled. He was especially fond of the older dealers who had worked for J.R. Watkins as young men.

E.L. King Sr. was the patriarch of the King family. He remained close to his brothers and sister, who often sought his advice on different matters. Pictured here from left to right are Durand C. Alexander, E.L. King Sr., Curtis King, Maude King Alexander, and Leroy King.

E.L. King Sr. was a shrewd businessman who built up his own personal empire in real estate, banking, and automobile dealerships. However, his ambitions sometimes landed him and the company on the wrong side of the law. Beginning in the 1930s, the King family and the J.R. Watkins Company were sued by the federal government for tax violations, drug-labeling violations, and violating rationing laws during World War II. E.L. King Sr. was forced to step down as president in 1944 and died five years later in 1949.

Bud King joined the company as an executive in 1935 at age 21. In 1941 he was made general manager of the company and succeeded his father as president of the J.R. Watkins Company in 1944. Bud is credited with putting several progressive ideas into effect under his presidency. He began giving tours of the Watkins Manufacturing Plant and Research Farm, expanded Watkins' agricultural product line, and began an employee profit-sharing plan.

Five

THE POST-WAR
YEARS

Watkins counter stores were also used as distribution centers for the vast sales force across the United States and Canada. Here Watkins salesmen and women pose for their photograph in front of an unidentified counter store.

Expansion had to be put on hold during World War II, but resumed once the war was over. In 1946 a branch was established in Johannesburg, South Africa. As sales grew, so did the need for more space. Pictured here is the new Manufacturing and Distribution plant that Watkins opened in 1957 at Springs, Transvaal, South Africa.

With the war over, Watkins resumed expansion into foreign markets by opening new branches in South Africa, New Zealand, and Australia. Here workers at a warehouse in Johannesburg, South Africa, are stacking cases of Watkins products.

Watkins Products Incorporated had salesmen and counter stores in every state, as well as U.S. territories. Here J.F. Mendez shakes the hand of a customer in front of the Watkins counter store in San Turce, Puerto Rico.

The post-war economic boom also allowed Watkins to expand and modernize its current branch offices and distribution centers. Pictured here is Watkins' Los Angeles branch office.

The Watkins administrative and manufacturing complex at Winona, Minnesota, sprawls across an entire city block. The ten-story manufacturing plant has dominated Winona's skyline for over 90 years.

At its peak, Watkins employed hundreds of office workers and managers in various divisions, such as city sales, the filing department, and the cost department.

In the age before computers, it was necessary to employ large numbers of clerks and secretaries in order to process orders and keep accurate records of sales, financial statements, and dealer information. This photograph shows the main office of the Montreal branch.

Designed by George W. Maher and built in 1913, the Memphis, Tennessee, branch office and manufacturing plant supplied Watkins dealers in the south and southwest with Watkins products. It would remain one of Watkins' largest branches until the late 1960s. The company eventually closed this branch and the United Warehouse and Terminal Corporation bought the buildings in 1971.

The Newark, New Jersey, branch of the J.R. Watkins Company continued to be the main manufacturing and distribution center for the company's products on the east coast. Shown here in the late 1940s, the Newark plant was responsible for producing Watkins Shredsope and other varieties of soap.

The manufacture of soap was a messy job, as seen in this photograph from the Newark, New Jersey, manufacturing plant. This kettle contained 300,000 pounds of boiling soap.

Here is another photograph taken at the Newark plant showing bars of hand soap being manufactured.

(*above*) This is a photograph of Ralph G. Boalt, in the second row at far left, posing with Watkins Dealers at a Watkins Convention in Raleigh, North Carolina, in August of 1955. Ralph was vice-president in charge of Farm Research and Overseas Foreign Operations. He married Mary Eleanor King in 1927 but they were divorced a few years later.

(*left*) The research conducted by entomologist Dr. Melvin H. Doner was instrumental in the success of Watkins' agricultural products during the 1940s and 1950s. Here Dr. Doner is sorting pyrethrum flowers at the Watkins lab in Winona, Minnesota.

The Watkins Research Farm was a national leader in animal feed research during the 1950s. It also served as a testing ground for other Watkins products such as fly sprays and insecticides. In this picture, cattle are being fed with the feed developed at the research farm.

As Watkins continued to expand its agri-products line, it also expanded the research farm by adding new barns, sheds, and silos. Each year, thousands of people were bussed out to attend tours of the farm. In the background is Kings Bluff Mansion built in 1942 by Mary King.

During the 1930s, jobs were scarce and becoming a Watkins salesman offered a chance for a steady income. After World War II, the American economy was booming and there was an abundance of jobs. The result was an aging sales force with fewer young men choosing a career as a Watkins Man. Pictured here is Arthur H. Senne of Elgin, Illinois, standing beside his delivery van.

The economic prosperity of the average American household during the decade after World War II brought continued growth to Watkins. The "Watkins Man" was still the most important factor in the successful selling of Watkins products. However, dramatic social changes of the late 1950s and 1960s would bring about the demise of the once-familiar Watkins door-to-door salesman.

The 1950s brought the arrival of the Interstate Highway System and the use of semi trucks as the principal method of transporting Watkins products across North America. The fleet of trucks and trailers operated out of the Watkins Agri-building on East 10th Street in Winona.

Beginning in the 1950s, Watkins became more aggressive in advertising its products. In this photograph, Phil Hansen, a Watkins salesman from California, holds a poster for Watkins Vitamins with Minerals.

Six

CHALLENGING TIMES IN
A CHANGING WORLD

Watkins continued to enjoy yearly sales growth through the mid-1950s. Shown in this photograph are city sales managers from across the country with signs displaying their sales increase for 1954. The entire increase of the City Sales Department was $663,831 in 1954. Clarence Currier headed the City Sales Department.

Beginning in 1955, Watkins began to see a yearly decline in product sales. In order to improve sales, the top executives at Watkins decided to implement a national advertising campaign by placing advertisements in nationally-published magazines such as *Reader's Digest*, *Ebony*, *Good Housekeeping*, *McCall's*, and the *Saturday Evening Post*. Shown here reviewing advertisements are Clarence Currier, Louis Goldberg (head of advertising), Bud King, Doug Robinson, and Ken Herberling.

In 1959, the J.R. Watkins Company changed its name to Watkins Products Incorporated. This was done to help modernize Watkins' image and was timed to coincide with its National Advertising Campaign. Here Elmer Ramsay of Waterbury, Connecticut, stands alongside his Chevrolet van holding his product carrier that proclaims that Watkins Products are "Nationally Advertised."

The new advertisements presented Watkins products in new packaging with young models displaying the products. This advertisement for Mary King Blue Crystal Shampoo ran in *Good Housekeeping* Magazine.

In the early 1950s, Watkins advertisements were often centered on the family and particularly the housewife. The new advertisements often depicted young women and hinted at a more glamorous singles' lifestyle.

Although still the main seller of Watkins products, the Watkins Man found it more and more difficult to make a living as a salesman. More women were beginning to work outside the home, creating competition from new companies such as Avon, and the emergence of grocery and retail chain stores were taking customers away from Watkins.

To help boost its new advertising campaign, Watkins began to use celebrities in their advertisements. In this advertisement, Mrs. Sugar Ray Robinson promotes Mary King Cosmetics.

"Birthdays needn't count against you"

says...

Mrs. Sugar Ray Robinson
wife of retired World's Middleweight Champion... outstanding stylist and hostess

Mary King Cosmetics," says Mrs. Sugar Ray, "well deserve their place of honor on my dressing table—and yours!" Your Watkins dealer today brings you a breath-taking new line of Mary King Cosmetics. You'll love SMART FINISH MAKE-UP, the glorious new liquid powder foundation which conceals tiny imperfections and tones the skin to a finer, clearer, youthful texture. Choice of four beautiful, flattering shades —Sunlight, Suntone, Suntone, Sunbrown.

Choose From The Complete Line of Mary King cosmetics—the finest quality... and at surprisingly moderate prices. Ask your Watkins Dealer about Mary King Face Powders, Creme Make-up, Creme Rouge and Lipsticks—other exciting Mary King cosmetics to help keep you looking your loveliest. Exquisitely packaged; perfect gifts.

Watkins Products

FROM THE WATKINS LABORATORIES
"THE SHOPPING CENTER THAT COMES TO YOUR HOM[E]"

Good Luck and Good selling Dave Garroway

To supplement the advertisements in national magazines, Bud King decided to advertise Watkins Products on national television. Beginning in 1960, Dove Garroway, the host of the NBC *Today Show*, advertised Watkins Products during commercial segments of the show. These prime-time advertisements were very costly to the company and failed to show a significant impact on sales.

With the retirement of Louis Goldberg in 1961, Herb Lockwood became the new vice president of Advertising. Here he is shown with Clarence Currier of the City Sales Department.

Along with its advertising campaign, the company also tried to regain lost sales by promoting its best-selling products through special offers. Pictured here are Harry Meyers, the vice president of Sales, Freeman Schroeder of Rural Sales, and Executive Frank Mertes looking at the final sale results of Watkins Gold Label Vanilla Special.

Despite the advertising campaign and product specials, sales continued to decline. By now Grace King and Mary Eleanor King felt that the time to sell the company had come and asked Ralph Boalt to negotiate with Charles Pfizer & Co. for terms of sale. Pfizer wanted 100 percent of all the shares of Watkins, but Bud refused to sell his 10 percent and the deal collapsed. Grace and Mary Eleanor then voted Bud out as president of Watkins.

Succeeding Bud King and becoming the first non-family president of Watkins was James Doyle. Doyle had previously worked for the A.T. Kearney Management consultation firm and had done a six-month study of Watkins. He recommended that Watkins should focus on cosmetics because Avon was making money in cosmetics at this time. He then convinced Grace King that he was the one who could return profitability to Watkins.

New colognes and perfumes were packaged under such names as Torch Song, House of King, and High Gear.

Switching to cosmetics placed an added burden on the company, which was already struggling financially. Retooling the manufacturing lines and the costs of marketing new products kept the company from realizing any profits. Despite its financial problems, it was business as usual at Watkins, which included continuing to provide tours of the manufacturing plant to interested visitors and civic organizations.

Watkins actively recruited young people to its sales force in an attempt to reach younger buyers and help bolster the company's modern image. Pictured here is Lee King, the oldest son of Bud King, recruiting a young college student to become a Watkins salesman.

Even though Watkins was successful in recruiting young salesmen, most would leave for other jobs after only a short period of time. Times had changed such that a person could no longer make a living as a door-to-door salesman. The result was devastating to Watkins as its sales force began to shrink at alarming rates.

To help new dealers, Watkins provided training sessions to teach successful selling techniques and to provide product education. Here is Craig Currier, the son of Clarence Currier, at a dealer meeting in Toronto, Canada, in 1965.

Although the emphasis of Watkins' advertising was on promoting cosmetics, the traditional Watkins food products such as spices, vanilla, and extracts continued to be the top product sellers for the company.

ATKINS MIN-VITE FOR WINE. A complete mineral, vitamin and antibiotic pre-mix formulated especially for swine.

SLANTOMATIC HOG OILER. Tough, economical, trouble-free. Can be mounted easily and quickly anywhere.

SARCOPTIC MANGE OIL. Controls both sarcoptic mange and lice on hogs. Can be used in Slantomatic Oiler.

FARM DISINFECTANT Destroys disease germs in buildings and on equipment. Use in farrowing barns, finishing lots.

OOSTER-PAK FOR WINE. Contains an antibiotic s vitamins. Use to prevent or at Bacterial Enteritis (scours).

DRY INSECTICIDE. Controls lice and acts as a deodorant. Use in hog houses, in bedding, or on hogs.

LINDANE CONCENTRATE. Mix with water, then spray hogs to prevent mange and lice. Can be sprayed inside the ear.

VITAMIN AID. Use in water or feed. Treats or prevents deficiencies in Vitamins A, D, Niacin Riboflavin and Pantothenic Acid

OG AND POULTRY POW-ER. Prevents or treats swine sentery or bloody scours. Add drinking water as directed.

PIG PRYMER. Pig Prymer supplies iron and copper necessary to prevent or treat iron deficiency anemia. Administered orally.

WORMER FOR SWINE AND POULTRY. Use either in feed or drinking water as directed. Does not set back production.

Watkins Agri-Division showed strong sales during the late 1960s with many popular products such as Watkins MIN-VITE pre-mix of minerals and vitamins for both hogs and cattle. All products were tested at the Watkins Research Farm.

Young salesmen like Larry Henson, shown here, were finding that most of their customers were middle-aged or older and had little interest in cosmetics. Most tended to buy products such as Watkins Vanilla and Watkins Cinnamon.

Despite the continued decline in sales, shrinking sales force, and rising production costs, James Doyle continued to believe that the future of Watkins was in cosmetics and beauty products. Pictured here is Georgine Modjeski working on the aerosol line.

The changes that Watkins experienced during the 1960s were not limited to new leadership and new products. The Administration Building that was built in 1911 needed to be updated. New energy-efficient windows were installed and the elegant but dim light fixtures were replaced with modern fluorescent lighting.

The new lights had a dramatic effect on the office area of the Administration Building. Desk lamps were no longer needed to help the straining eyes of office workers.

New lighting was not the only modern technology implemented at Watkins. A new Honeywell computer system was also installed to keep track of new orders, billing, and other records.

The use of computers improved efficiency and eliminated the need for large numbers of office workers. Pictured here are keypunchers who were responsible for accurately entering orders and billing information into the new computer system.

In early 1968, Watkins began to prepare for its Centennial Celebration, including a large celebration at the company picnic in June. The year began with the mayor of Winona, R.K. Ellings, signing a city proclamation declaring 1968 Watkins Centennial Year. Standing behind him is Watkins President James N. Doyle.

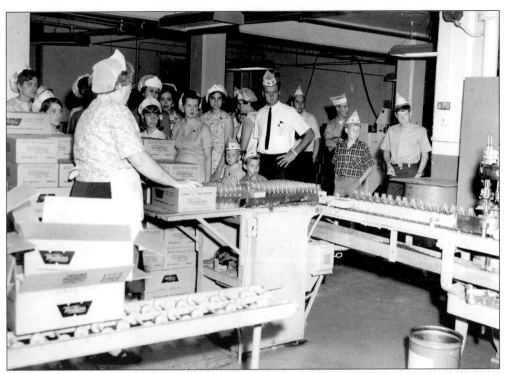

Watkins continued to give tours of the Administration Building and manufacturing plant as part of its Centennial Celebration. During its open house on June 14, 1968, over 2,000 people toured Watkins. In this picture, a Watkins employee explains her role on the bottling line.

The Centennial Celebration also coincided with Steamboat Days. The recently crowned Miss Winona, Jan Wiest, and her attendants, Nancy Sievers and Ann Werner, are shown here holding Watkins Heirloom Cologne Mist during their tour of Watkins. Nancy Sievers was the daughter of Watkins Executive Vice-President E.J. Sievers.

The Watkins Picnic in June of 1968 would be the grand finale of the Centennial Celebration. Local and state dignitaries were invited to the ceremony that was held on the campus of St. Mary's College. Watkins President James Doyle is shown here standing in front of the Holiday Inn marquee.

Watkins President James Doyle addresses a crowd of more than 2,500 employees and their families at the centennial day ceremony and picnic held at St. Mary's College.

Watkins picnics have always been family-oriented. Games and other fun activities were organized at the centennial picnic for children. After the games, the children were treated to Watkins punch and ice cream cones.

By the end of the 1960s, Watkins had undergone many changes as it attempted to modernize its products and its image. The most important and long-lasting change to Watkins was its loss of thousands of dealers during this time. With the disappearance of the Watkins salesman and the company's failure in the cosmetic market, darker days for Watkins were looming as the 1960s gave way to the 1970s. Pictured here is Earl Phillips, a city dealer from Illinois.

Seven
THE END OF
FAMILY OWNERSHIP

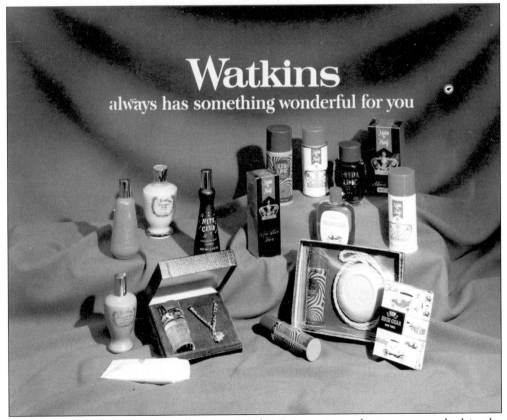

Despite six years of aggressive marketing, Watkins' cosmetic products never resulted in the profits that James Doyle believed they would achieve.

Many of Watkins' employees began working for the company right out of high school or college and have stayed with the company for decades. Pictured while working in the mailroom are Jerry Trocinski and Duane Evans. Evans later became vice-president of Finance.

Archie Trimm began working for Watkins in 1940 in the shipping department and is shown here 30 years later packing products for shipment.

By 1970, Watkins was struggling to remain solvent. To save money, Watkins closed its counter stores across the country and began to consolidate its manufacturing and distribution centers. This reduced shipping costs and saw the end of Watkins' fleet of trucks.

In an attempt to generate revenue, Watkins began to do contract manufacturing. Betty Schugort is shown here filling tubes of PANA toothpaste.

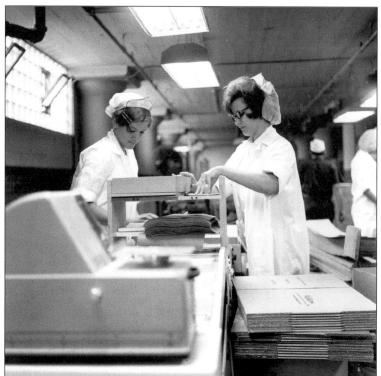

Despite its difficult financial situation, the employees of Watkins continued to remain loyal to the company and optimistic about the future.

Christmas was a favorite holiday at Watkins. The beautiful lobby of the Administration Building seemed to have been built with Christmas in mind. In this image, employees string lights around the tree.

The early 1970s saw the retirement of several long-time employees who had been with the company since the early 1920s. Elmer Sievers was the last of the senior management staff to retire. He began at Watkins in 1923 as an office boy in the accounting department and retired in 1971 as the executive vice president of Watkins.

In 1933 Chester McCready joined his brother, Kenneth McCready, at the Watkins Printing Plant, and like his brother he stayed with Watkins for 40 years.

Evan "Tubby" Beynon was one of Watkins' most colorful personalities. After joining Watkins in 1928, he remained with the company for 42 years. Tubby was a graduate of the New York Academy of Fine Arts and began his career at Watkins by designing product labels. He later designed and did the artwork for Watkins' calendars and almanacs, but was well-known around the company for the sometimes risqué birthday and get-well cards that he drew for fellow employees.

The Watkins Research Farm played an important role in Watkins' history for over 35 years—however, by the end of 1971, Watkins had decided to close the farm and sell off the animals, equipment, and property. The cashed-strapped company could no longer afford to keep the farm operation going, and the sale of the farm would bring the company desperately-needed cash. Cy Crawford is pictured above with one of the thousands of visiting tour groups, and below, farm workers are seen feeding the last herd of beef cattle raised on the research farm.

Despite seven years of losses, cosmetics and colognes continued to be emphasized in Watkins catalogues for 1971.

Popular Watkins products like Watkins Four Season Beverage Mix, Watkins Black Pepper, and Watkins Cinnamon were found in the back of the catalogs and rarely given any emphasis within the catalog.

At the end of 1971, Watkins posted a loss of $1.4 million, which was the seventh straight year that Watkins had posted a loss in sales. The decision to manufacture cosmetics and colognes had been a disaster for Watkins right from the beginning. In order to raise capital to keep the company going, Watkins sold its overseas operations and assets in Australia, New Zealand, and South Africa, closed its domestic counter stores, and sold once-valuable branch manufacturing offices such as those in Memphis, Newark, Oakland, and Denver.

In 1972, Bud King, who was still chairman of the board, fired James Doyle and installed his son David King as the new president of Watkins. David had been with Watkins since 1962 and had been in charge of Canadian operations prior to being appointed president.

Fred King, left, is shown here with retired Watkins employee Howard Bauman and Dr. Lewis Younger. Fred was appointed vice president of Watkins to help his brother run the company. (Courtesy of the Winona County Historical Society.)

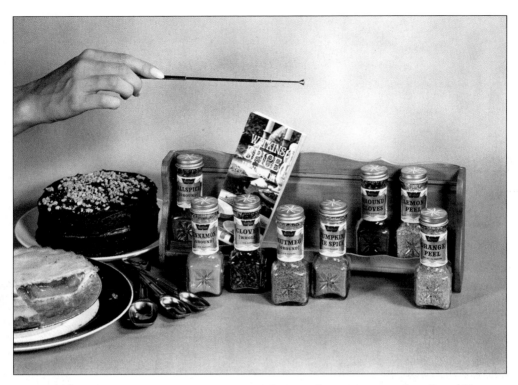

Realizing that the company was not going to make it in the cosmetic market, David King set out to return Watkins to its roots. Manufacturing and marketing emphasis was again given to Watkins' food products such as spices, extracts, and beverage mixes.

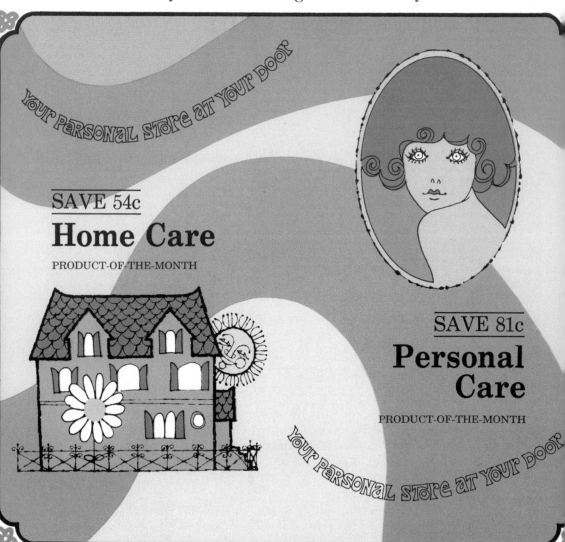

In the early 1970s, Watkins again tried to get a new generation of young people to become consumers of Watkins products. During this period, Watkins also set about to update its appearance to reflect the images and styles of the younger market. This 1973 catalog cover is an example of the advertising style of the time.

Most of Watkins' product labels and packaging dated from the early 1960s, when the company had changed its name from J.R. Watkins Company to Watkins Products Incorporated. Pictured here are the old and new bottles of Watkins extracts. The new bottles are unique to Watkins extracts and are still used today.

Along with repackaging products, Watkins also set about to streamline the number of products it sold. Some products were dropped due to poor sales and others due to changing environmental laws.

Having closed and sold off the other manufacturing plants and most other distribution centers, the Watkins manufacturing plant in Winona was now the sole producer of Watkins products and the main distribution center. Besides losing other manufacturing and distribution centers, Watkins also lost employees. Even the Winona plant saw a decline in workers as people began to leave to seek different jobs.

For those that stayed with the company, there was still a sense of teamwork and enjoyment.

In the mid-1970s, Watkins did begin to see an increase in sales again after a decade of losses. In another marketing attempt to help sales, Watkins introduced the J. Zachary line of gourmet food products and the Liberty Street products. Products offered under the J. Zachary name were gourmet popcorn, mustards, and salad dressing.

The company did not want this line to be associated with the Watkins name. To accomplish this, all orders were sent to a Rollingstone, Minnesota, address.

The J. Zachary line ultimately failed because of poor name recognition, and because it never created a new market for its products. These products were also expensive when compared to other brand names like Watkins.

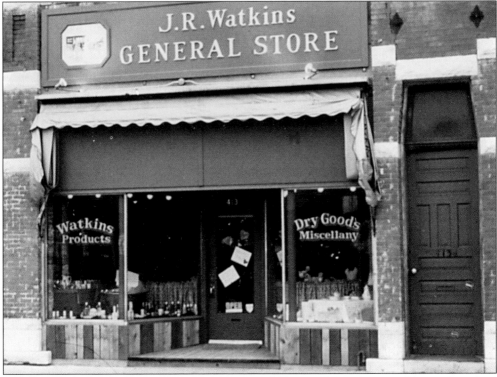

In 1974, Fred King wanted to see if Watkins could successfully return to the retail market. Watkins opened a store at 413 Jay Street in La Crosse, Wisconsin. The store was given an old-time general store theme and offered a variety of merchandise besides Watkins products.

The store resembled an antique shop, rather than a Watkins counter store. Watkins products seemed to receive little emphasis and were placed in the background away from the public. The store did poorly and was closed within a short time.

In this 1978 photograph, Ann Messenger and Rhonda Hanson present two unidentified Watkins associates with a new microwave oven that was offered as a sales incentive. By 1978, all the ideas and incentives that David and Fred King tried had failed to significantly change the financial situation of the company. By the end of the summer, creditors were beginning to call in the loans that had been given to the company. The company filed for bankruptcy and Irving Balto replaced David King as president of Watkins. Balto was able create a financial plan acceptable to Watkins' creditors; however, it was rejected by the federal bankruptcy judge.

Eight

A New Beginning

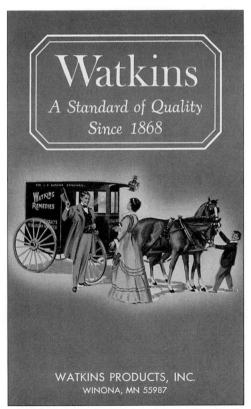

On December 27, 1978, Minneapolis entrepreneur Irwin Jacobs bought Watkins Products Incorporated and thus ended 110 years of family control over the company. Jacobs' acquisition of Watkins offered a new beginning for the company.

Irwin Jacobs was born and raised in Minnesota. After he graduated from North High School in Minneapolis in 1959, he went on to work for Northwestern Bag Corporation, which his father owned. By age 37 he had become a successful businessman, owning such companies as Larson Boats and Minstar Incorporated. After buying Watkins, he was determined to turn the company around.

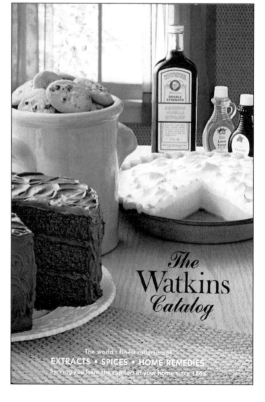

Beginning in 1979, Watkins decided to return to its roots and concentrate on spices and food products ending its 14-year emphasis on cosmetics. This shift is evident in Watkins catalogs. For years, spices, baking products, and extracts had been placed in the back of catalogs; they were now featured on the cover and front pages of the catalogs.

Although a large number of employees left Watkins during the mid- and late 1970s, the company did retain a core group of longtime employees who believed that they could help return Watkins to profitability. This photograph was taken shortly after Irwin Jacobs took control of Watkins.

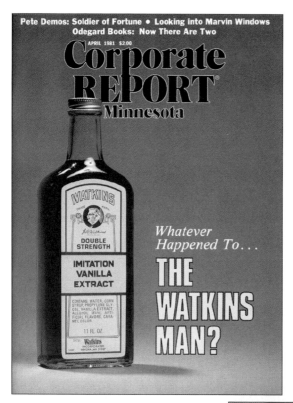

Pete Demos: Soldier of Fortune • Looking into Marvin Windows
Odegard Books: Now There Are Two

APRIL 1981 $2.00

Corporate
REPORT
Minnesota

*Whatever
Happened To...*

THE
WATKINS
MAN?

In 1981, Watkins was the subject of the cover story in the April edition of *Corporate Report Minnesota* magazine. The article chronicled the decline of Watkins and also reported on the company's status since Irwin Jacobs took over. The article notes that from 1979 to 1981 the number of Watkins dealers increased from 5,000 to over 16,000.

Over the years, Watkins has produced numerous publications for both its associates and employees. In the early 1980s, a new company magazine was published called *The Watkins World*. This magazine would be used to inform dealers of company goals, products, and upcoming events such as Watkins conventions.

IRWIN JACOBS
WATKINS PRESIDENT

The resurgence of Watkins began with associates like Ed and Sue Williams. The Williams decided to become full-time dealers for Watkins after attending the 1981 Watkins Convention. The Williams felt that they could succeed because of the product quality, rich company heritage, and the sales support that Watkins offered. Ed and Sue felt that Watkins offered them freedom to be their own bosses and an opportunity to achieve higher rewards. By 1995 they had become directors and achieved Grand Master status with Watkins. By achieving Grand Master status, the Williams received a $100,000 bonus from Watkins.

The year 1993 was a milestone in the history of Watkins, as the company celebrated its 125th Anniversary. The company was recognized once again by both local and state civic leaders. The main celebration was held at Winona Senior High School and attracted 15,000 people over a five-hour period. The center display consisted of 11,430 frosted cupcakes that were later given away. A Watkins cook-off was the main event of the celebration. Posing with Irwin Jacobs are cook-off contestants Ellen Burr, Carolyn Popwell, Robert Lee Bolender, Gladys Earl, and Cheryl Thompson. Ellen Burr won the contest with her recipe for Royal Pork Medallions entrée featuring Watkins Royal Pepper, Watkins Chicken Soup Mix, and Watkins Onion Liquid Spice.

In January of 1996, Mark Jacobs joined the Watkins as the vice president of Sales and Training Development. In 1998 he was made president of Watkins. Mark moved to Winona in 1995 with his wife, Tricia. After a successful acting career, appearing in the hit movies *Biloxi Blues*, *Goodfellas*, *Trusting Beatrice*, and *Bleeding Hearts*, Mark realized that the company needed a long-term plan and set about to establish one that would guide the company over the next five, 10, and 20 years. He has also set out to establish brand awareness by introducing select Watkins products into the retail market.

In 1996, Bill Porter was recognized at the Watkins International Business Conference for his 30-plus years as a Watkins salesman in Portland, Oregon. Despite suffering from cerebral palsy, Porter became the top retail salesman in all of Oregon, Idaho, Washington, and California for several years. He is seen here with his long-time friend, Shelly Brady.

In 2001, award-winning actor William H. Macy starred in a movie about Bill Porter's life called *Door to Door*. This movie details Porter's real-life experiences as a Watkins Man, including the triumphs and professional success he achieved despite his cerebral palsy. The inspirational movie won six Emmys, is frequently broadcast on cable television, and is currently sold at video stores as well as the Watkins website.

Some of the most elegant things come in black.

In 1995, Watkins Black Pepper and Watkins Cinnamon celebrated their centennial anniversary. Both of these spices continue to be top sellers for Watkins and are sought out for their superior quality.

Some of the most exciting things come in red.

Watkins has begun to expand into commercial markets by offering gourmet quality products to food services at bulk prices. Products such as Watkins Vanilla, Watkins Black Pepper, and Watkins Cinnamon are just a few of the products available to restaurants, hotels, and cafeterias.

Watkins now offers non-profit organizations such as the D.A.R.E. program the opportunity to sell Watkins products as a fundraising endeavor.

Watkins offers its associates many incentives and rewards for their success in selling and promoting Watkins products. For top-selling associates, trips to such exotic places as Cancun, Barbados, and New Zealand have been used as incentives. These images depict the Cancun resort where Watkins associates stayed (*above*) and the mountains of New Zealand (*right*).

In this photograph, Watkins President Mark Jacobs and his wife, Tricia, (back row, far left) pose with top Watkins associates during an incentive trip to New Zealand.

Although Watkins is best known for its vanilla and spices, the company's personal care products are also gaining a reputation of their own. Watkins offers a popular line of personal care products featuring Aloe Vera.

Want to simplify your life? Move to Winona, Minnesota.
(Or just send for our free grapeseed oil.)

It seems everyone is trying to slow down these days. We've never felt that way in Winona. Tucked quietly away in Minnesota's river valley, our little town has a way of putting one at ease. Even the mighty Mississippi turns placid here. So it's no wonder J.R. Watkins set up shop here 133 years ago — selling homemade remedies from a horse-drawn wagon. Products made from simple, pure ingredients that just made life better.

More than great vanilla.

While we're known best for our vanilla (it earned gold medal honors at the 1928 Paris World Expo), we offer an incredibly wide range of products. From gourmet spices, to personal care items, to supplements — even earth-friendly cleaning supplies. In fact, our steak sauce recently garnered high praise from the folks at GQ magazine.

We've known what women want since 1868.

Whether it's our tried and true Petro Carbo Salve or SoyNilla, our latest vanilla concoction, Watkins has always known how to pamper women. To us, there's nothing new about new age. It's not about hype or gimmicks. Just natural stuff that works. All made to the highest standards — our own. Okay, so you probably won't be moving here any time soon. At least you can evoke the feeling every time you use one of our products.

THE FIRST ONE'S ON US.

Receive a free 12.7 oz. grapeseed oil with your first purchase. Call 1-800-WATKINS for a free catalog, or visit us at www.WatkinsOnline.com. Mention code CP601.

WATKINS
TRADE MARK
MAKING THE EVERYDAY EXTRAORDINARY SINCE 1868

As Watkins enters the 21st century, it continues to manufacture a large variety of cooking, personal care, health, and cleaning products. This 2001 advertisement offers shoppers an opportunity to receive a free bottle of Watkins Grapeseed Oil with a customer's first purchase.

Watkins began as a family company in 1868 and continues as a family company as it passes the quarter-century mark under the ownership of Irwin Jacobs. Pictured here are three generations of the Jacobs family: Mark, Alexander, and Irwin.

Since its earliest days, Watkins products have been brought directly to the home, first from a traveling Watkins salesman, later by catalogs, and today through the Internet. Modern technology allows customers to order directly from their homes just by visiting the Watkins website at www.watkinsonline.com.

Today Watkins' mainline catalog and website offer over 350 products, such as spices, cooking products, cleaners, and personal care products. Many of these products such as Watkins Menthol Camphor Ointment and Watkins Pudding Mixes have been favorites with consumers for generations.

Beginning under Irwin Jacobs' leadership and continuing under that of Mark Jacobs, Watkins has seen strong growth in both sales and consumer demand for its products. Irwin and Mark Jacobs are shown sitting in a restored 1929 Model A delivery truck inside the lobby of the Watkins Administration Building. (Courtesy of Steve Woit/*New York Times*.)

Anti-Aging Botanicals

Beginning in early 2004, selected personal care products will be available in retail stores. These new Anti-Aging Lotion products use a blend of six botanical ingredients: Cornflower Extract, Linden Extract, Matricaria Extract, Hypericum Extract, Calendula Extract, and Chamomile Extract to moisturize and nourish skin.

GRAND EXCURSION 2004™

Grand Excursion 2004™

The 150th anniversary of the 1854 Grand Excursion is an exciting time to be a part of the Upper Mississippi River community. The route from Rock Island to St. Paul is one of the most scenic areas in America, with vibrant cities, quaint river towns and scenic bluffs offering a unique travel experience.

Each town along the way has its own flavor to add and an opportunity to show its pride. To help with this worthy cause, we are proud to offer high-quality Watkins products—made right here along the Mississippi River since 1885. A portion of the sales of these fine products will go toward your community's efforts in promoting this event.

▲ Mississippi Mud Cocoa Set
Enjoy a traditional mug of cocoa like you've never had before! Includes Watkins Pure Cocoa in a lined burlap bag; a 2-oz bottle of Watkins Original Double-Strength Vanilla and a recipe card packed in a commemorative Grand Excursion 2004™ mug.
04935 $16.49

▶ Original Double-Strength Vanilla®
Watkins Vanilla is made from the world's finest Madagascar Bourbon vanilla beans. Our secret low-alcohol, double-strength formula is more flavorful than regular vanilla extracts in recipes requiring baking or freezing. In our original glass Trial-Mark Bottle with gift carton.
01002 (325 mL/11 fl oz) $17.99

During the summer of 2004, Watkins joined river towns all along the upper Mississippi River in celebrating the 150th anniversary of President Millard Fillmore's Grand Excursion up the Mississippi River in 1854. Watkins was the largest corporate sponsor of the 2004 Grand Excursion.

Watkins now offers a new opportunity to enjoy its products at home through its Good Tastings program. This program allows friends and family to taste the quality of Watkins products through featured recipes.

The reputation of Watkins products remains unsurpassed after 135 years. The determination to only sell the highest-quality products ensures that Watkins customers will continue to receive the best products on the market.

The future of Watkins can be found in its past. The traditions of quality products and customer service that began with J.R. Watkins in 1868 continue today and will be just as recognizable 100 years from now.